Skyler

Skyler, grade 2

"SO MANY GODS,
SO MANY CREEDS,
SO MANY PATHS
THAT WIND AND WIND

WHILE JUST
THE ART OF BEING KIND
IS ALL THIS SAD WORLD NEEDS."

~ Ella Wheeler Wilcox

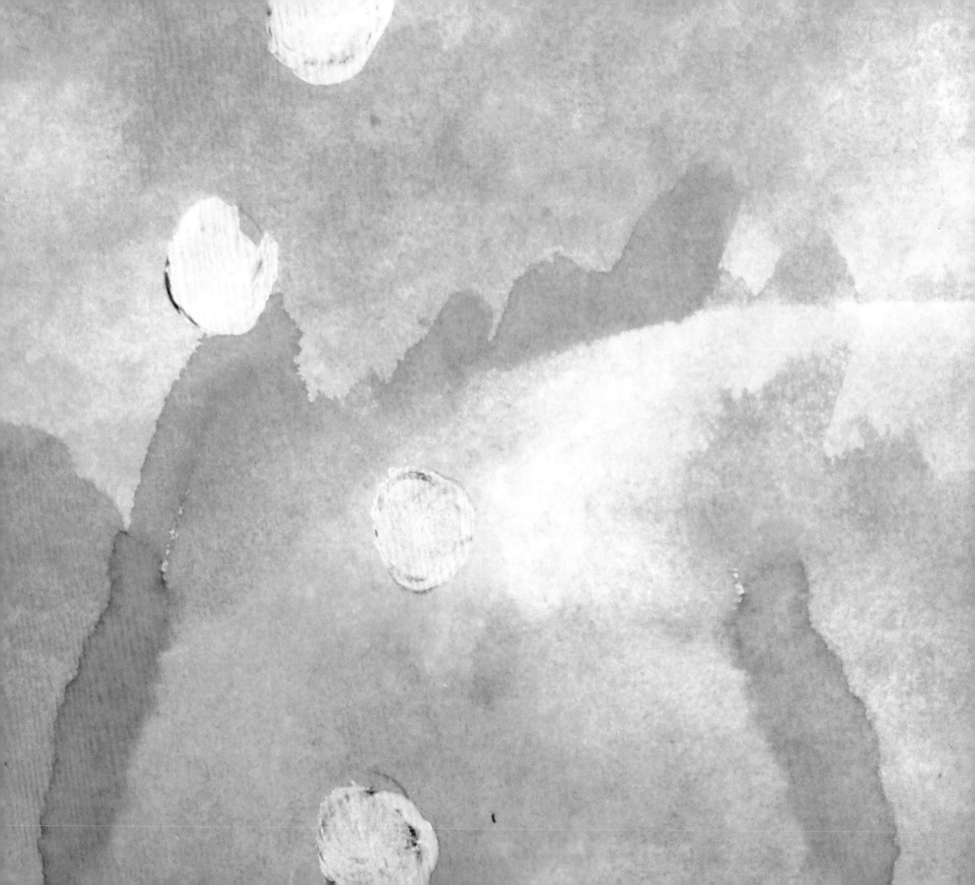

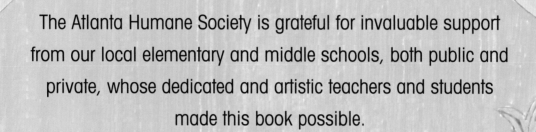

The Atlanta Humane Society is grateful for invaluable support from our local elementary and middle schools, both public and private, whose dedicated and artistic teachers and students made this book possible.

Lilly, grade 4

atlanta hu♥ane society

Published by Hermes House Press Atlanta, GA, USA 30319 www.hermeshousepress.com
Produced by Interface Graphics, Inc. Minneapolis, MN 55401 www.igigraphics.com

ISBN-13: 978-0-9825503-1-1

Library of Congress Control Number: 2009939221

Manufactured in the United States of America
1 — BP — 12/15/09

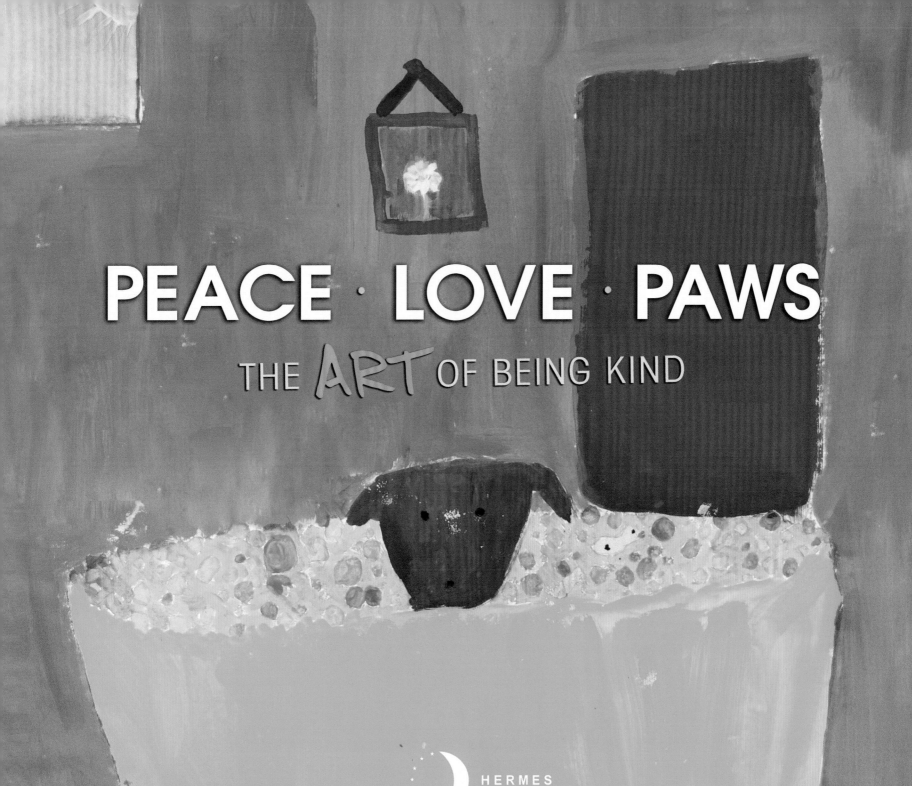

PEACE · LOVE · PAWS

THE ART OF BEING KIND

HERMES

Madelaine, grade 7

"HORSE SENSE IS THE THING A HORSE HAS WHICH KEEPS IT FROM BETTING ON PEOPLE." ~W.C. Fields

Yazmine, grade 6

EVERYBODY NEEDS A FRIEND

When we began our Be Kind to Animals art contest nearly 30 years ago, the children of Atlanta responded by painting their hearts out for their pets. As a result, our halls were bedecked with a delightful assortment of brightly colored dogs and cats - sprinkled with a rabbit or hamster here and there. Over the years, however, a subtle change began to occur and gradually the contest took on a life of its own. Out of the blue, a stray peacock or penguin would appear, followed by a polar bear one year and a giant purple squid the next! But when a hedgehog made its way through our doors and into our hearts, we knew there was more to the story than a group of children dabbling in paint. They were sending us messages from the animal kingdom!

Children and animals alike have an uncanny ability to remind us of those invaluable lessons we once learned and have somewhere left or misplaced along the way: simple truisms like "fences keep pets safe" and "everybody needs a friend." They also have the unique ability to teach us to forgive and to help us heal, especially when a broken heart is involved. And they have the power to show us that while the world may appear to be a chaotic mess, there still remains a mysterious order, an unspoken beauty and a deeper meaning in all of it and all of us. All we need to do is open our hearts.

Between these pages you will find words of wisdom, scenes of "pure happiness," whispers and warnings, and unfettered displays of affection. We hope you find comfort, joy and humor in this artful anthology presented to you by the youth of Atlanta and above all, we hope it inspires you to widen your circle of compassion to include all beings.

Peace. Love. Paws: *The Art of Being Kind* benefits the work of the Atlanta Humane Society, the oldest private non-religious charitable organization in Atlanta and one of the oldest humane agencies in America. We are a regional sanctuary for animals, pet owners, and the public concerning animal welfare issues and problems, and provide a safe haven for unwanted and abandoned pets, with no time limits on finding a new forever family for them. Our board of directors, staff, trained professionals and volunteers speak for those who cannot speak for themselves.

It is our mission "to prevent neglect, abuse, cruelty and exploitation of animals and to assure that their interests and well being are fully, effectively and humanely protected by an aware and caring society"- a mission established with the founding of the Society in 1873. Over the years the Society efforts have included championing women's rights, universal suffrage, and the establishment of child labor and protection laws in Georgia and the nation. Enjoying a successful history of accomplishment, the Society has developed support programs addressing the needs arising from the human/animal bond in combination with the core programs of animal welfare. With utmost dedication and integrity to this promise, the Society has successfully advanced animal welfare in our community, in our state, and in the Southeast as a voice for the voiceless.

Peace. Love. Paws.

The Atlanta Humane Society 2009

Emma, grade 7

Katelyn, grade 4

Kaitlyn, grade 2

Tiane, grade 4

Caroline, grade 5

Kamren, grade 3

Zaynah, grade 7

Ian, grade 1

THE ART OF BEING KIND

Established in 1915, "Be Kind to Animals Week" is the nation's oldest nationally-celebrated week. During the heyday of Progressivism in turn-of-the-century America, the humane movement (pertaining to humans as well as animals) erupted as social justice issues came to the fore. Providing help for "those who could not speak for themselves" became a cause close to many people's hearts. The creation of "Be Kind to Animals Week" helped push the cause into the classrooms, and allowed the humane movement to take hold with children.

"Be Kind to Animals Week" is celebrated in shelters nationwide in many ways. For nearly 30 years the Atlanta Humane Society has celebrated this important week with an art contest for elementary and middle-school students. The contest draws 600-1,000 entries every spring from children who submit original drawings or paintings depicting what being kind to animals means to them. Finalists are invited to an awards ceremony where they are feted with prizes and recognition in a room where their work is displayed "art gallery" style. Parents and teachers (and the public) have the opportunity to buy the artwork with a small donation to the Atlanta Humane Society. Some of the artwork successively ends up in a permanent gallery in our adoption area.

The contest is a great way for the children in the community to express their love and concern for the animals with whom they share their lives, as well as animals they may never see except in a zoo or on television. It's also a great way for their work to make a difference educating visitors to the AHS. Themes include pets, wild animals, destruction of habitat, leash laws, spay/neuter, puppy mills, concern for animals nobody loves, cruelty prevention, and more. Artwork is judged on originality, message, artistic presentation and ability, and theme.

The "Be Kind to Animals Week" Student Art Contest is one of the highlights of my work at the AHS, and I am always amazed at the creativity and vision of these young artists. I hope you will be, too. Your purchase of this book supports our efforts and supports the arts. Thank you.

Mailey E. McLaughlin, M.Ed.
Contest Coordinator
Behavior, Training, and Education Coordinator
Atlanta Humane Society

"THE ZOO IS A PLACE
FOR ANIMALS TO STUDY
THE BEHAVIOUR
OF HUMAN BEINGS."

~ Unknown Author

Please Save The Amur Leopard. And Please Don't Kill Them.

Anyuan, grade 4

Diana, grade 1

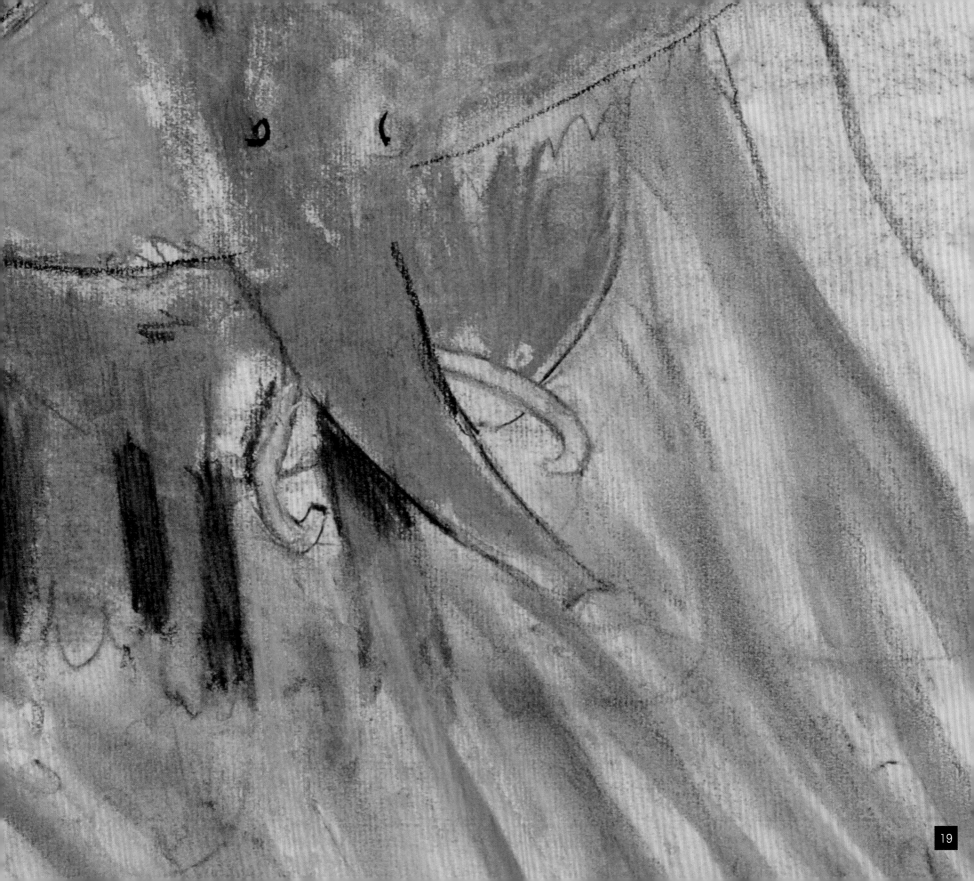

Jessica, grade 3

Daniel, grade 7

Antonella, grade 5

Bailey, grade 1

Carmella, grade 4

Carina, grade 8

Mia, grade 7

Stephanie, grade 7

Zoe, grade 6

28   Kasey, grade 7

"A BIRD DOES NOT SING BECAUSE IT HAS AN ANSWER. IT SINGS BECAUSE IT HAS A SONG." ~ Chinese Proverb

Megan, grade 6

Emily, grade 2

Let Your Pets Have Freedom

Leila, grade 4

India, grade 7

Savannah, grade 8

Caitlin, grade 2

Peter, grade 1

Pablo, grade 2

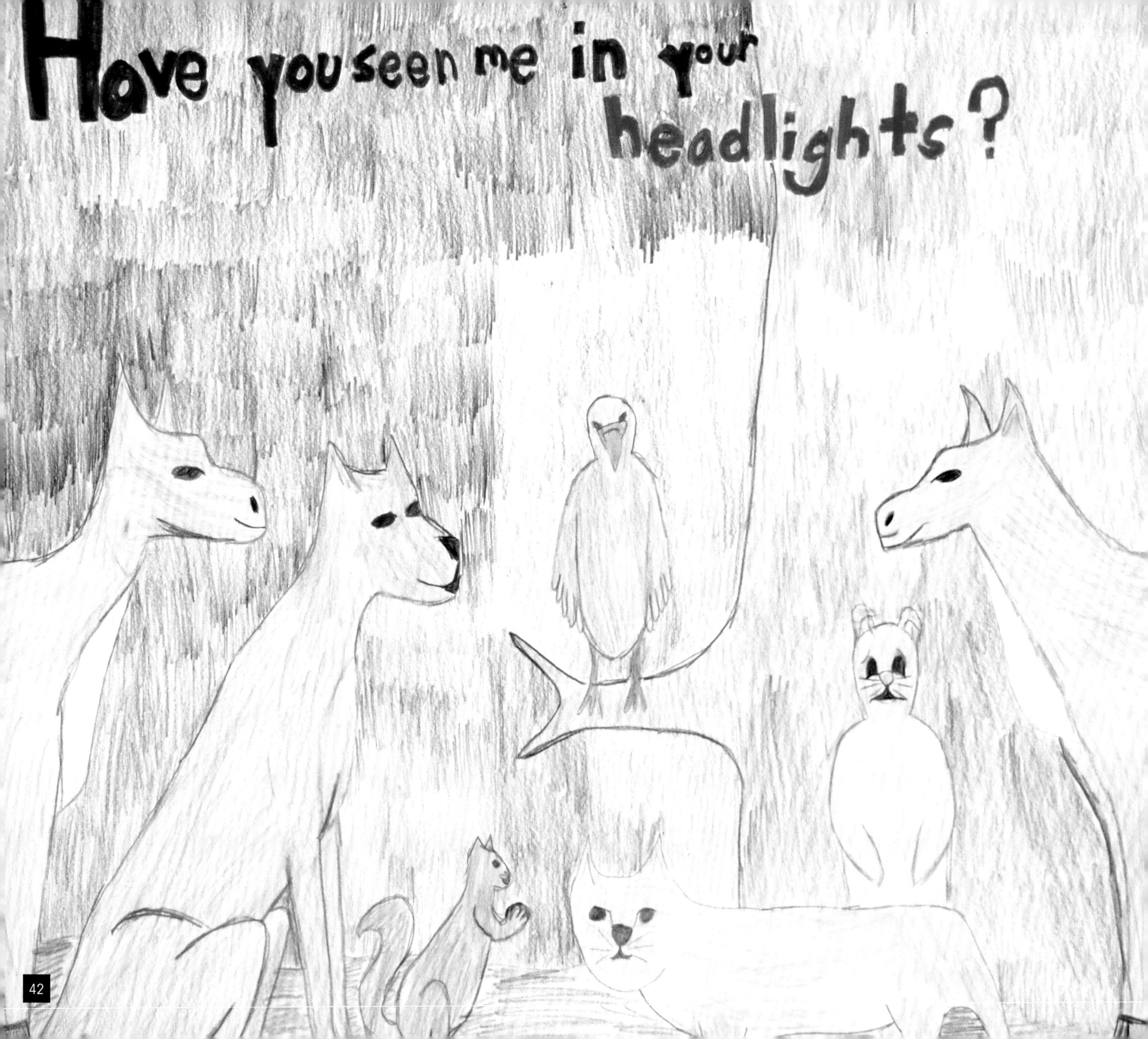
Have you seen me in your headlights?

Apryl, grade 5

"ALL ANIMALS ARE EQUAL BUT SOME ANIMALS ARE MORE EQUAL THAN OTHERS."

~ George Orwell

Bianca, grade 4

Bianca York

Ariel, grade 7

Kristin, grade 6

Dylan, kindergarten

Charlotte, grade 2

Bruno, grade 1

Maia, kindergarten

Stephen, grade 7

Amphibians

Lee, grade 6

"WE CAN JUDGE
THE HEART OF A MAN
BY HIS TREATMENT
OF ANIMALS." ~ Immanual Kant

Andrew, grade 1

Alexandra, grade 5

George, grade 3

Daniel, kindergarten

Paige, grade 1

Rachel, grade 6

Dustin, grade 6

Jenna, grade 3

Never harm Wildlife

Hikema, grade 3

Ashleigh. grade 4

Be Kind to Animals

Help them Along their way

Scott, grade 8

Butterflies Love flowers!

Neyda, grade 3

Kierra, grade 5

Amy. grade 3

Peyton, grade 1

Brittany, grade 4

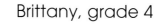

Jeri, grade 8

Amanda, grade 2

Go To The Vet To Get Your Pet Checked And Vaccinated

Avery, grade 2

"A DOG HAS LOTS OF FRIENDS BECAUSE HE WAGS HIS TAIL AND NOT HIS TONGUE."

~ Unknown Author

Meredith, grade 7

73

Yommi, grade 2

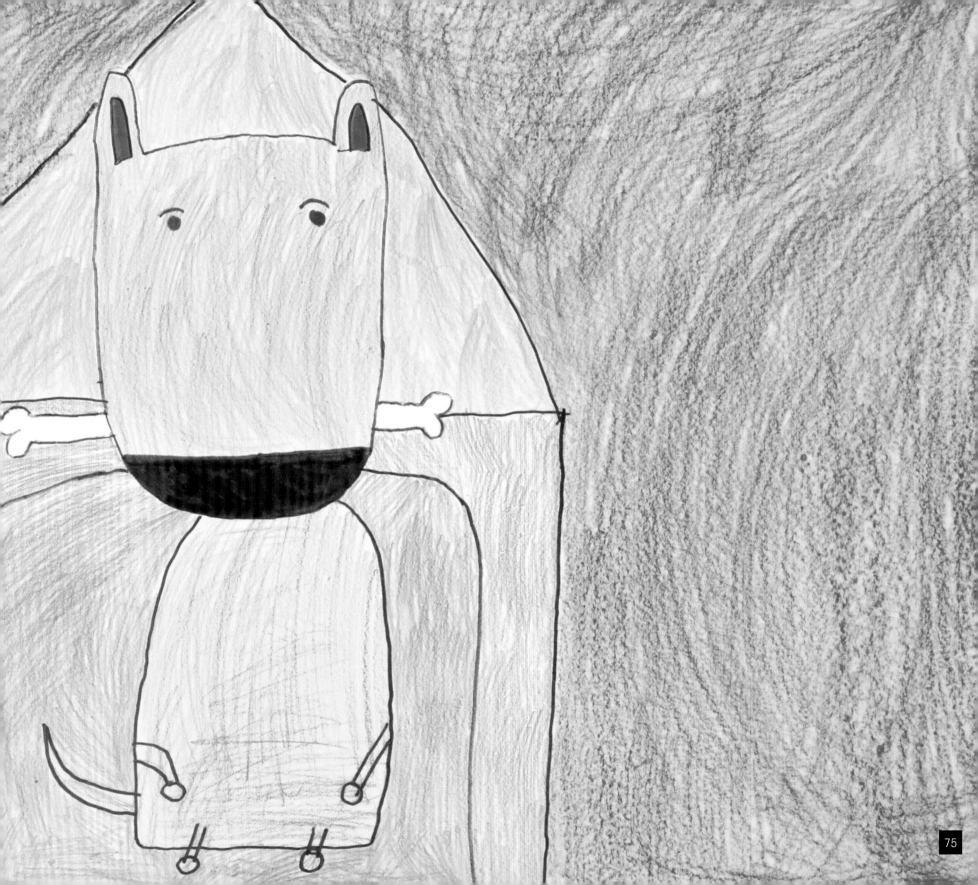

take me ho

Sam, grade 8

Jordan, grade 6

Sidney, grade 7

Jordan, grade 7

81

Mary, grade 5

Liz, grade 7

Adam, grade 6

Never send a dog away, keep them until they are old and gray.

Samantha, grade 8

Rose, grade 8

A well fed Pooch!

Sara, grade 4

Maya, kindergarten

Keep Dogs Happy

"A CAT IS A PUZZLE FOR WHICH THERE IS NO SOLUTION."

~ Hazel Nicholson

Gracie, grade 1

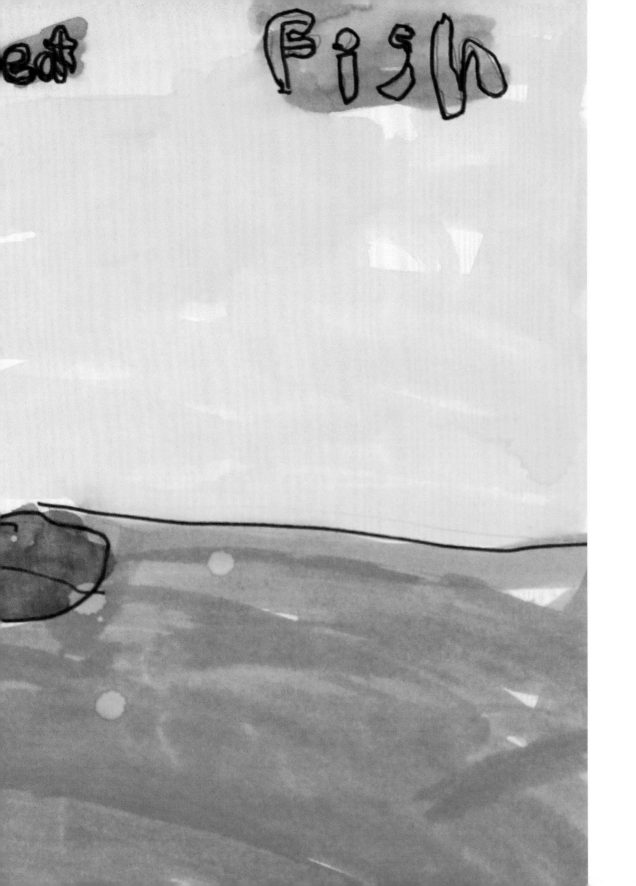

Andrew, kindergarten

Jair, grade 7

Anna, grade 1

If you feed your cat
Catnip your cat will play with you

Alexandra, grade 7

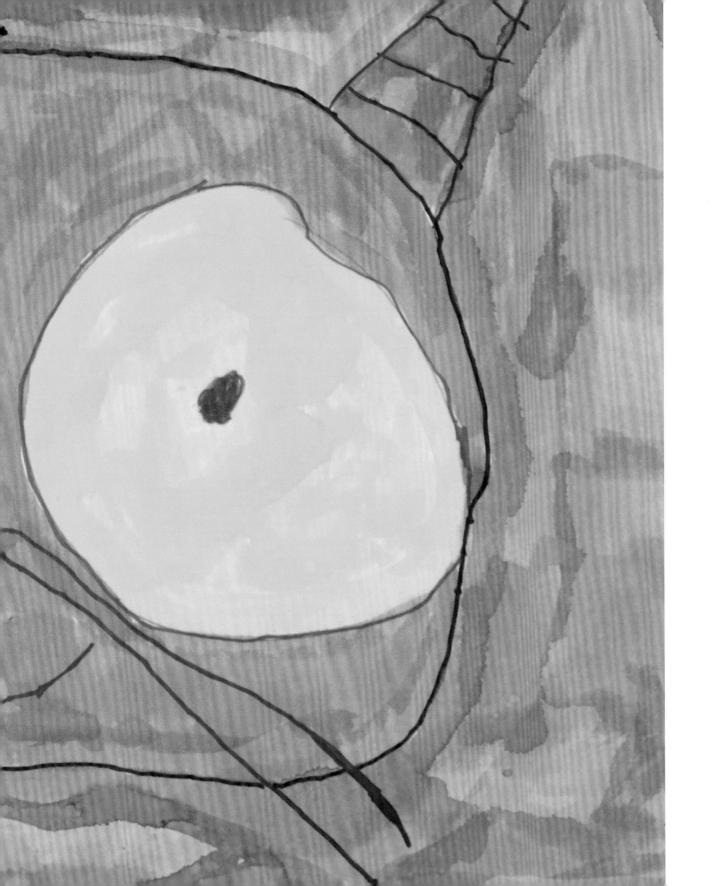

Karthik, grade 2

Madelyn, grade 4

Katie, grade 4

Megan, grade 5

"LOTS OF PEOPLE
TALK TO ANIMALS....
NOT VERY MANY LISTEN,
THOUGH....
THAT'S THE PROBLEM."

~ Benjamin Hoff, The Tao of Pooh

Liam, grade 2

Liam Gross

Be Nice To Hedgehogs

Dont Throw plastic 6 pack rings into

ocean!

Matthew, grade 1

Maddie, grade 5

Kendall, grade 3

Oliver, grade 7

DO Not Harm Sharks!

Victor, kindergarten

KEEP OUR WATER CLEAN

Adam, kindergarten

113

Emily, grade 7

Averi, grade 5

"I THINK ANIMAL TESTING IS A TERRIBLE IDEA; THEY GET ALL NERVOUS AND GIVE THE WRONG ANSWERS."

~ Unknown Author

Brianna, grade 7

Anneliese, grade 3

Bria, grade 5

Yuri, grade 8

Margot, grade 4

"LOVE THE ANIMALS.
GOD HAS GIVEN THEM
THE RUDIMENTS OF THOUGHT
AND JOY UNTROUBLED."

~ Fyodor Dostoyevsky

Gavin
McElroy

Erin Collins

Alice, grade 7

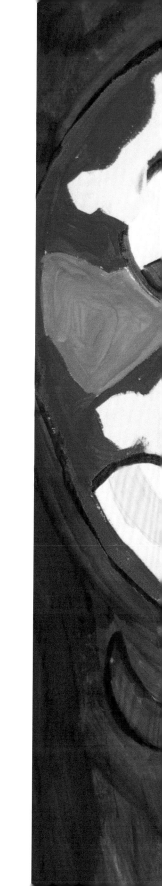

Love
The

127

Jenna, grade 7

Maura, grade 5

Jeawon, grade 8

Morenke, grade 5

Clair, grade 2

Amanda, grade 7

Michelle, grade 7

139

HOW YOU CAN HELP

The Atlanta Humane Society and Society for the Prevention of Cruelty to Animals, Inc. was founded in 1873 and is the city's oldest, private, not-for-profit animal welfare organization. Originally chartered to help women and children as well, the AHS now focuses its efforts on addressing the pet overpopulation problem and encouraging pet adoption in Georgia.

The Atlanta Humane Society offers numerous programs and services in addition to pet adoption. Located in Midtown Atlanta, we welcome and encourage support from the public. We welcome volunteers and invite people of all ages to get involved with our community-wide events and attend fundraisers for our rescued pets. We also welcome your generous contributions that allow us to continue to provide emergency pet rescue, adoption services, and programs to the community. To learn more, please contact us at 404.875.5331.

A VOICE FOR THE VOICELESS

We are grateful for the invaluable support we receive from our volunteers, staff, board of directors and countless visitors whose compassion for unwanted, neglected and abused animals has contributed - beyond word and measure - to our mission at the Atlanta Humane Society. We especially owe a debt of gratitude to the children of Atlanta who have given us the gift of **Peace. Love. Paws: *The Art of Being Kind***.

Martin Luther King, Jr. once said, "Occasionally in life there are those moments of unutterable fulfillment which cannot be completely explained by those symbols called words. Their meanings can only be articulated by the inaudible language of the heart."

We hope the children of Atlanta have touched your heart.

Peace. Love. Paws: *The Art of Being Kind* benefits the work of the Atlanta Humane Society and is a reminder to all of us that there is no greater art than the art of being kind.

To purchase additional copies of this book, visit us at www.atlantahumane.org or www.hermeshousepress.com.

Artwork from this page: Top Row (L to R) Laren, grade 6, John, grade 5, Asa Alexandra, grade 3, Hallie, grade 2, Sophia, grade 1, Martina, grade 7, James, grade 7, Heather, grade 8, D. Maitland, grade 7, Tramauh-Teasha, grade 7, Jasmine, grade 7 Bottom Row (L to R) Leslie, grade 1, Rachel, grade 5, Alex, grade 8, James, grade 1, Meghan, grade 3, Joseph, kindergarten, Eric, grade 4, Sumiya, grade 7, Katherine, grade 3, Claire, grade 5, Bryan, grade 6

Artwork from page 125: Row 1 (L to R) Caroline, grade 5, Gavin, grade 2, Catherine, grade 3 Row 2 (L to R) Ashley, grade 5, Shelby, kindergarten, Tiana, grade 4 Row 3 (L to R) Lauryn, kindergarten, Ceara, kindergarten, Karen, grade 7 Row 4 (L to R) Jenna, kindergarten, Erin, grade 3, Anna, kindergarten

Artwork from back cover: Top Row (L to R) Neel, grade 2, Alexandra, grade 7, Caitlin, grade 2, Madelaine, grade 7, Shelby, kndergarten, Jahadic, grade 2 Center : Marc, grade 6   Bottom Row (L to R) Skyler, grade 2, Kristin, grade 6, Ansley, grade 5, Lauryn, kindergarten, Andrew, kindergarten, Oliver, grade 7